The Saving Name *of* God the Son

by Jean Ann Sharpe

Illustrated by the Artwork of
Fra Angelico

BETHLEHEM BOOKS • IGNATIUS PRESS
Bathgate San Francisco

In the beginning

was the WORD,

and the WORD—who

was *with* God and

who *was* God—

became

flesh . . .

and dwelt among us.

The Son of Man

come

down

from

heaven,

to serve and to give his life . . .

as a ransom for many.

For in him was life

and the life was

the LIGHT of men:

a LIGHT TO

THE NATIONS

shining . . .

in the darkness.

Behold,

he is the LAMB OF GOD

who takes away

the sin of the world.

Anointed by the Spirit . . .

He is the

Beloved Son,

calling the Bride to the

Marriage Supper

of the Lamb;

giving to her the

most precious gift,

his Body and Blood,

sacrificed . . .

on the

wood of

the cross:

Our Lord Jesus Christ!

The Son of God,

our Savior and

Redeemer,

descended

into hell,

and on the

third day . . .

he rose again

from the dead.

He is

the RESURRECTION

and the LIFE,

the TRUTH

and *our* WAY . . .

to the

Father.

Ascended into heaven, he is
our HEAD, our SOURCE,
and HIGH PRIEST
of the good things
to come.

He is seated
at the right hand . . .

of God,

the Father

Almighty.

Jesus Christ,
King of Glory,
Eternal Judge,
Bright Morning Star

He is coming again.

Amen.

Come, Lord Jesus, *come!*

Art and Text References

Works and references are listed below in the order in which they appear in the book, beginning with the cover art.

The Virgin enthroned, infant Jesus and saints, (Madonna delle ombre); Fra Angelico (1387-1455) • Mural, 193 x 273 cm • Location: Museo di S. Marco, Florence, Italy Photo Credit: Erich Lessing/Art Resource, NY

See: Acts 2:21, 28; 4:12 and *The Catechism of the Catholic Church*: 430-451; 2665-2666

Cortona Altarpiece with the Annunciation, without predellas; Fra Angelico (1387-1455) • Location: Museo Diocesano, Cortona, Italy • Photo Credit: Scala/Art Resource, NY

See: John 1:1, 14; Luke 1:26-38 and *The Catechism of the Catholic Church*: 148; 241; 291; 423; 484; 490; 494; 2617

Nativity; Fra Angelico (1387-1455). From the doors of the Silver Cabinet. Ca. 1450 • Location: Museo di S. Marco, Florence, Italy • Photo Credit: Scala/Art Resource, NY

See: Luke 2:1-20 and *The Catechism of the Catholic Church*: 525; 1159

Adoration of the Magi; Fra Angelico (1387-1455). From the predella of the Linaiuoli altarpiece, 1433-1435 • Location: Museo di S. Marco, Florence, Italy • Photo Credit: Nicolo Orsi Battaglini/Art Resource, NY

See: Matthew 2:1-16 and *The Catechism of the Catholic Church*: 528

Baptism of Christ; Fra Angelico (1387-1455). Ca. 1440-1445 Fresco • Location: Museo di S. Marco, Florence, Italy • Photo Credit: Scala/Art Resource, NY

See: Matthew 3:13-17 and *The Catechism of the Catholic Church*: 535-537; 719-720

Communion of the Apostles (Institution of the Eucharist); Fra Angelico (1387-1455). From the doors of the Silver Cabinet. Ca. 1450 • Location: Museo di S. Marco, Florence, Italy • Photo Credit: Nicolo Orsi Battaglini/Art Resource, NY

See: Matthew 26:26-28; Mark 14:22-24; Luke 22: 19-20 and *The Catechism of the Catholic Church*: 610-618; 1328-1332

Crucifixion; Fra Angelico (1387-1455). From the doors of the Silver Cabinet. Ca. 1450 • Location: Museo di S. Marco, Florence, Italy • Photo Credit: Nicolo Orsi Battaglini/Art Resource, NY

See: Mark 15:24-38; Luke 23:33-46; John 19:18-37 and *The Catechism of the Catholic Church*: 616-618; 623

Christ's Descent into Limbo; Fra Angelico (1387-1455). From the doors of the Silver Cabinet. Ca. 1450 • Location: Museo di S. Marco, Florence, Italy • Photo Credit: Nicolo Orsi Battaglini/ Art Resource, NY

See: 1 Peter 3:18-20 and *The Catechism of the Catholic Church*: 632-635

Christ resurrected; the three Marys at the tomb; Fra Angelico (1387-1455), 1438. Mural, 181 x 151 cm • Location: Museo di S. Marco, Florence, Italy • Photo Credit: Erich Lessing/Art Resource, NY

See: Matthew 28:1-8; Mark 16:1-7; Luke 24:1-7 and *The Catechism of the Catholic Church*: 639-641

Ascension of Christ; Fra Angelico (1387-1455). From the doors of the Silver Cabinet. Ca. 1450 • Location: Museo di S. Marco, Florence, Italy • Photo Credit: Nicolo Orsi Battaglini/Art Resource, NY

See: Luke 24:50-53; Acts 1:9-14 and *The Catechism of the Catholic Church*: 659-661, 668

The Last Judgment. Christ in his glory, surrounded by angels and saints; Fra Angelico (1387-1455). Fresco (ca. 1436) • Location: Museo di S. Marco, Florence, Italy
Photo Credit: Erich Lessing/Art Resource, NY

See: Matthew 25:31-34; 24:30-31 and *The Catechism of the Catholic Church*: 671; 673; 680

Graphic Design: Marie Leininger
Art director: Roseanne Sharpe

First paperback printing: May 2018

ISBN: 978-1-932350-84-5
Library of Congress Control Number:
2009927796

Bethlehem Books • Ignatius Press
1194 Garfield St S
Bathgate, ND 58216
www.bethlehembooks.com

Printed in the USA by New Hope Publications

Nihil Obstat:
Msgr. Joseph Goering

Imprimatur:
† Samuel J. Aquila, D.D.
Bishop of Fargo

May 24, 2009
Feast of the Ascension of the Lord

Special thanks to our friends at the *Maryvale Institute*, *St. Martin de Porres Dominican Community* and *Ignatius Press*